Where Is
the Vatican?

by Megan Stine

illustrated by Laurie A. Conley

Penguin Workshop

For my dear friend Betsy and her children and grandchildren: Geoff, Anne, Paula, Michael, Delaney, Kendall, Garrison, and George—MS

For Brian, for his endless support—LAC

PENGUIN WORKSHOP
An Imprint of Penguin Random House LLC, New York

Library of Congress Control Number: 2019030855

ISBN 9781524792596 (paperback)   10 9 8 7 6 5 4 3 2 1
ISBN 9781524792602 (library binding)   10 9 8 7 6 5 4 3 2 1

Contents

Where Is the Vatican?

It was a cold, wet day in March 2013. Crowds of Catholics filled a huge square outside the largest church in the world: St. Peter's Basilica. More than fifty thousand people had come to find out who would be the next pope.

The answer depended on a vote that was taking place inside a chapel beside the huge church. One hundred fifteen cardinals were locked inside to vote for the new pope. (Cardinals are the most important Catholic priests after the pope.) To be elected pope, one of the cardinals had to receive two-thirds of the votes. The cardinals wrote the name of the person they were voting for on a piece of paper. They kept their votes secret by disguising their handwriting. After being counted, the ballots were burned and smoke drifted up from the chapel.

The results of the votes are always announced to the world in a puff of smoke. White smoke means that a new pope has been elected. Black smoke means that no one has gotten enough votes yet.

On the first day of voting, no one was chosen. Black smoke billowed out of the chapel chimney. The same thing happened the next morning—black smoke. The cardinals would have to vote again.

Rain began to fall. Still, the crowds remained, waiting under umbrellas into the night.

Finally, on the evening of March 13, a plume of white smoke floated up into the air. The crowd burst into joyous cheers. They waved flags from countries all over the world. Then bells began to ring and ring, announcing that a new pope had been chosen.

By the time Pope Francis appeared on the balcony overlooking the square, the rain had

stopped. He spoke humbly to the crowds, asking them to pray for him. He knew he had a big job ahead of him.

Being pope meant he would head the Catholic Church, all the world over. As pope, he would also be the leader of a country. It is the smallest country in the world, located entirely inside the city of Rome, Italy.

The country is called Vatican City.

CHAPTER 1
A Safe Place for Christians

How did Vatican City become the smallest country on earth?

The answer lies in the story of Christianity— a story that began more than two thousand years ago when Jesus was alive.

The Christian religion is based on the teachings of Jesus and the events of his life. Christian people believe he is the son of God. Jesus was killed by the Romans for his preaching. He was nailed to a cross and left to die. Christians believe he rose from the dead three days later and returned to God in heaven.

For a long time after that, it wasn't safe to be a Christian—especially in Rome. Rome was the center of power in the ancient Roman Empire. One leader of the empire was Nero. Nero didn't want a new, different religion taking over his world. He wanted everyone to obey him and pray to the Roman gods the way they always had. He killed many Christians.

Nero

St. Peter

Peter was one of Jesus's followers. He wouldn't give up his new religion. So he was crucified, too. According to the story, his body was buried right where he died in Rome.

Christians loved and admired Peter for his faith and courage. As time went on, he became known as St. Peter, the first bishop of Rome. A bishop is someone chosen to lead the church.

For the next three hundred years, many Christians were threatened, tortured, and harmed. But an emperor named Constantine took over the Roman Empire in the fourth century. Constantine believed in the Christian religion. He declared that people should be allowed to worship whatever religion they chose.

Constantine donated lands and churches to the Christians. He gave the bishop of Rome a palace to live in, called the Lateran Palace. One of the earliest Christian churches, called St. John Lateran, was built beside the palace. From then on, the bishop of Rome was called the pope, and all the popes were called the bishop of Rome. "Pope" comes from the word *papa*, which means *father*. For the next thousand years, all the popes lived in the Lateran Palace.

Emperor Constantine

Priests, Bishops, Cardinals:
What's the Difference?

Priests are ministers in the Catholic Church. Each priest is usually in charge of just one church, or parish. Bishops are priests who have been chosen by the pope to watch over several churches in a small area called a diocese (say: DYE-uh-sess).

Priest   Bishop

An archbishop is in charge of a larger area or a big city, called an archdiocese. Cardinals are bishops who have been appointed for special duties by the pope. The pope appoints the cardinals to give him advice, help run the Vatican, and to choose a new pope when a pope dies or retires.

Cardinal

Lateran Palace

At the same time, Constantine began to build another huge church. Construction lasted from AD 360 to 380. He called it St. Peter's Basilica. It was built very near the site where St. Peter was buried. It was located on a hill near the Tiber River, on a spot called Vatican Hill.

Old St. Peter's Basilica

What's a Basilica?

A basilica is a type of church or other building with a long central chamber, a door at one end, and a raised platform at the opposite end. The longest part of the church, where people come to worship, is called the nave. At the far end of the church is a semicircular spot called the apse. Sometimes the apse is under a dome. The altar is usually tucked into the apse, but St. Peter's Basilica is different. St. Peter's is laid out in the shape of a cross. The Papal Altar is at the center of the cross.

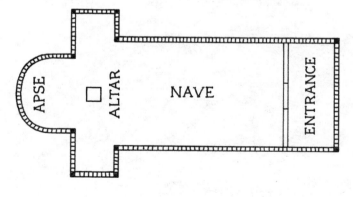

As time went on, the popes gained more and more power throughout Europe. Starting with Constantine, many emperors gave fabulous gifts to the church. In return, the popes often acted as peacekeepers when foreign tribes attacked Rome. Popes were often treated as if they had equal power to emperors, kings, and queens. They ruled over large areas of land—called the Papal States—in what is now Italy. (Italy didn't become the country as we know it today until 1870.)

Map of Italy, 1815–1870

But often, the popes and the Vatican were under attack from tribes who stole many treasures.

In the ninth century, Pope Leo IV had a huge wall built around the buildings that are now known as the Vatican. This was for protection. The wall was like a fortress—twelve feet thick and forty feet high. It had towers and windows that were really just small slits. From behind the openings, men could defend the Vatican by shooting arrows at attackers below.

Having a wall around the Vatican helped. It was the first step in creating a small city that belonged only to the church, where the pope could be safe.

But the wall didn't stop all the rivalries and violence. Before Christian leaders would be truly safe, they were going to need a bigger wall.

CHAPTER 2
Struggles for Power

Throughout the Middle Ages—the period from the 400s to the 1500s—church leaders struggled for power. Sometimes the pope's power was threatened by kings. At other times, popes were challenged by rival bishops.

One pope led an army into battle in order to survive. Another pope was thrown into prison by his rivals. Sometimes, a group of church leaders would get together and elect a new pope— even before the current pope had died. Then there were two popes at once, fighting for control of the church! There is also a story that in 882, Pope John VIII was poisoned and beaten to death. In 904, Pope Leo V was thrown into his own dungeon and strangled to death.

All the infighting gave the church a bad name. Finally, in the year 1049, a pope came along who wanted priests to be more devoted to their religion. Pope Leo IX created new rules.

He said priests couldn't marry or have children. Other popes made rules to make sure popes were not chosen by kings or emperors. They had to be elected by the cardinals.

Pope Leo IX

It was a good rule, however, the cardinals did not always agree. In 1268, Pope Clement IV died in the town of Viterbo, in Italy. The cardinals gathered there to vote on a new pope. But the voting went on for three years! Finally the leaders of the town decided to force them to vote. They locked the cardinals in the pope's house. When they still didn't choose a new pope, the town's leaders took away some of their food. Then they took more food. Then they removed part of the roof! At last, the cardinals chose Pope Gregory X.

Cardinals outside Pope Clement IV's home

Gregory X issued an order, called a Papal Bull. It spelled out more rules for electing popes. He said that in the future, cardinals would always be locked in a room in the palace where the pope had died. Food would be passed to the cardinals through a small opening. If they didn't choose a pope within three days, they'd get less food. Their pay would be cut short as well. The system of locking the cardinals up to choose a new pope is called a conclave.

Papal Bulls

In the past, when a pope issued a decree or order, he signed it with his seal to prove the decree truly came from him. The seal was a metal stamp that the pope pressed into a blob of melted lead or gold, leaving an imprint. The Latin word for blob is *bulla*, so the decrees became known as Papal Bulls.

Papal Bull from Pope Alexander IV, 1261

By the 1300s, the church had regained much of its influence and power in the world. Popes and cardinals crowned kings who were friendly to the church. In return, the kings often protected the pope and his lands.

The popes also excommunicated (that means kicked out of the church) kings who gave them trouble. A person who is excommunicated can't be part of the Catholic religion anymore.

Henry VIII

Henry VIII was king of England and a Catholic. (Nearly all Christians at the time were Catholics, but the word "Catholic" wasn't used until later.) By church law, Catholics were not allowed to divorce. But Henry VIII wanted to divorce his wife since she hadn't given birth to any sons. The pope refused, however. So the king decided to break away from the Roman Catholic Church. He started his own church, called the Church of England, and named himself the head of it. When the pope found out, he excommunicated the king.

Henry VIII and his second wife, Anne Boleyn

But the Vatican still wasn't always a safe place for every pope. In 1305, the new pope, Clement V, felt in danger due to political violence. So he built a papal palace in southern France where the French king would protect him. For the next sixty or seventy years, all the popes lived in France, afraid to return to Rome. When they finally did, they found the city in terrible shape. The Lateran church was in shambles, its roof caved in. The Lateran Palace had burned down in 1361.

Popes' Palace in Avignon

If the popes were going to live in Rome, it was clear the buildings would need updating to make them safer and better suited to the leader of the Christian world. Luckily, some very wealthy popes came along who wanted to breathe new life into the church's ancient buildings.

CHAPTER 3
The Vatican Is Reborn

St. Peter's Basilica, at the heart of the Vatican, was now a thousand years old. The palace at the Vatican was old, too. Both were in terrible shape. And neither one had the beauty of the buildings that were springing up to the north of Rome in a city called Florence. So, over a period of many years, the popes decided to rebuild and replace the buildings.

Nicholas V, who became pope in 1447, had been to Florence when he was young. He hired the best, most well-known artists from there and brought them to Rome. He created a new library and stocked it with as many as five thousand books. But he died before he had a chance to fix up St. Peter's Basilica.

The popes who came after Nicholas decided that, rather than rebuild the old church, they would tear it down. They wanted a whole new St. Peter's Basilica built on the same site.

By 1481, a chapel was built beside the old cathedral. It was called the Sistine Chapel. The name *Sistine* comes from the name of Pope Sixtus IV, who had it built. The Sistine Chapel is the place where the cardinals now meet for the conclave—the secret meeting to elect a new pope.

The first stone for the new St. Peter's was laid in 1506. It took 120 years to complete St. Peter's Basilica. Seven chief architects worked on it and nineteen popes served through the construction.

At one point, the brilliant artist Michelangelo was put in charge of St. Peter's. He designed the huge dome for the basilica, using ideas from a number of different artists and architects.

Michelangelo was also chosen to decorate the ceiling of the Sistine Chapel. He painted nine well-known scenes from the Bible. One shows the serpent in the Garden of Eden. Another depicts the flood and Noah. The most famous picture shows the creation of Adam, with God reaching out his finger to touch Adam's hand, giving him life.

It took four years for Michelangelo to finish the job. He worked on the ceiling standing on a wooden platform high above the floor. His head was tilted far back at an angle and paint dripped on his face. It was hard work, but the results were glorious. Today, it is one of the most visited spots in the Vatican.

Other brilliant artists worked on the Vatican buildings, too. The Apostolic Palace was built as a place in which the pope would live.

Apostolic Palace

The Renaissance

At certain times throughout history, there is a burst of energy, or a flowering, in the arts. The 1400s in Florence, Italy, was one of those special times. Artists and writers created beautiful paintings, buildings, and marble sculptures such as the world had never seen. It was a rebirth of art and culture—a period we now call the Renaissance (say: REN-nuh-sahnce). *Renaissance* means *rebirth*. The popes and the church paid for much of the art that was created at that time.

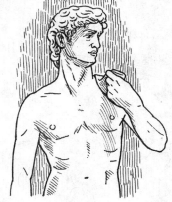

Michelangelo's statue of David

An artist named Raffaello Sanzio, called Raphael, was chosen to decorate the pope's apartment. He spent twelve years painting the walls of four rooms. Besides biblical figures and heroes of the church, some of the great thinkers of ancient times are shown—men like Plato and Aristotle—who are remembered for their ideas. Known as Raphael's Rooms, they are now open to the public as part of the Vatican museum tour.

Raphael's Rooms

Another palace, built by Donato Bramante, had a spiral staircase that led into a tower from the courtyard below. Bramante designed it as a ramp with very high ceilings. Why? So that the pope could ride his horse all the way up to the top!

Gian Lorenzo Bernini, a sculptor and architect, later designed the huge oval plaza in front of St. Peter's. Some of the marble for St. Peter's and other Vatican buildings was taken from the Colosseum! The Colosseum was the huge ancient Roman arena where wild animal battles and gladiator fights had been held.

But all the art and all the marble and stone needed to build St. Peter's were expensive. Pope Leo X, who was elected in 1513, decided to raise money by selling "indulgences." Indulgences were sort of like a "get out of jail free" card for sinners. In exchange for money, Pope Leo forgave people for committing sins. Otherwise, he said, they might be kept out of heaven.

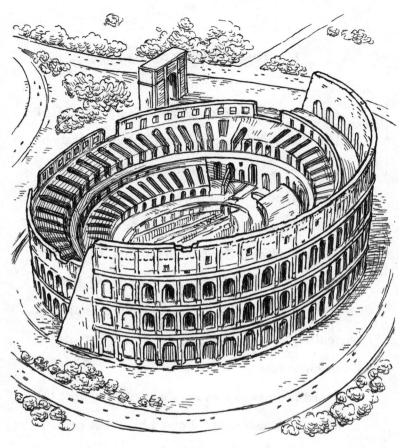

The Colosseum

Some people thought that the church selling favors was a terrible idea. They felt the pope had lost his way. So they broke away from the church.

Martin Luther (1483–1546)

Martin Luther was a German priest who turned against the church in Rome. He thought the sale of indulgences was wrong. Only God could forgive sins. In 1517, he wrote a long letter about his beliefs and sent it to a bishop. In the letter, he listed ninety-five problems with the church along with ways to change or reform it. According to some stories, he then nailed the list to the door of a church in Wittenberg. Pretty soon, copies of the list spread throughout Europe.

Martin Luther's ideas were a *protest* against the church. So people who followed his ideas became known as Protestants. After that, the church in Rome was called the Roman Catholic Church to set it apart from Protestants and other groups.

Although the Vatican was being rebuilt, the pope still wasn't entirely safe. In 1527, an army of angry soldiers marched into Rome. They sacked the city and looted the Vatican, taking everything they could carry. Pope Clement VII had to flee for his life.

It would take another four hundred years before the Vatican would become completely safe from attack—and become a separate country at the same time.

CHAPTER 4
A New Country Is Born

The Vatican was growing in size and becoming a place of tremendous beauty. But the popes had no real army of their own and no way to protect their property. Their power depended on keeping other kings and rulers happy.

In 1870, another army came marching into Rome.

This time it was an Italian army!

The takeover of Rome, 1870

Italy was becoming a unified country at last. The new leaders wanted Rome to be the capital city. But that meant taking control of land that had been ruled by the Catholic Church. The new Italian government offered to let the pope keep the part of Vatican City that was inside the wall. In exchange, the pope had to give up other lands. The pope refused. Instead, for the next fifty-nine years, he and three popes after him remained trapped as "prisoners" in the Vatican.

Signing of the Lateran Treaty
between Italy and the Vatican, 1929

Then, in 1929, Pope Pius XI made a deal with the leader of Italy, Benito Mussolini. They signed a treaty—an agreement—that created a new country, the State of Vatican City. It was a city-state—a very small country that is just one city. (There are two other city-states in the world today: Singapore and Monaco.)

As part of the agreement with Mussolini, the pope was allowed to keep control of several buildings that were outside the Vatican, including the Lateran Palace, St. John Lateran church, some offices, and two other large cathedrals.

The Vatican also kept Castel Gandolfo. It is a large palace south of Rome where the popes often live in the summer.

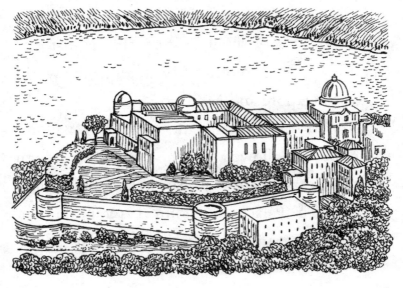

Castel Gandolfo

Once the Vatican became a country, it needed all the things a country has—its own money, its own post office, its own government, and its own flag.

All those things would come eventually—when the Vatican entered the modern world.

Benito Mussolini (1883–1945)

Benito Mussolini was the leader of Italy for more than twenty years. He was elected as prime minister in 1922, but three years later he took total control over the country and ruled as a dictator. Like Adolf Hitler in Nazi Germany, Mussolini used secret police to get rid of enemies. In 1940, Mussolini joined World War II on Germany's side. Italy and later Germany were both defeated by a group of countries led by the United States, Great Britain, and the Soviet Union. Mussolini was shot to death by his own countrymen at the tail end of the war.

CHAPTER 5
The Largest Church in the World

The stroll across the open plaza in front of St. Peter's is awe-inspiring. Ringed with 284 columns, the plaza itself is enormous. It's as long as three and a half football fields! More than three hundred thousand people can gather there. Statues of 140 saints stand atop the columns.

In the center of St. Peter's Square stands a tall, square, tapered column of marble with a pointed

Obelisk in
St. Peter's Square

top. It is called an obelisk and was brought from Egypt in AD 37. In 1585, nine hundred men and at least seventy-five horses worked for many months to move the heavy stone to where it stands now.

Straight ahead of the obelisk are the main doors of St. Peter's. Visitors and worshippers usually enter here. But once every twenty-five years, the beautiful bronze Holy Door on the far right is opened. Decorated with sixteen cast bronze panels, the Holy Door is really two doors that are, by tradition, sealed from the inside—with cement! They can only be opened in a Jubilee Year—a year of religious celebration for Catholics.

In 2016, Pope Francis declared a special Jubilee Year. After the cement was removed, he opened the doors himself in a ceremony that was seen by thousands. The pope walked up and knocked on the doors with a special hammer. When the doors were opened, it meant that the faithful were invited to pass through to reach God. Each person who enters through the Holy Door in prayer is forgiven for their sins.

At the end of the Jubilee Year, the Holy Door is sealed again. A fancy gold trowel is used to apply a layer of the cement.

No matter what door a visitor goes through, the inside of St. Peter's Basilica is overwhelming. The size of the church alone is difficult to take in. Brass markers on the floor show the length of other big churches compared to St. Peter's. The markers show that St. Peter's is longer than any other.

St. Peter's Basilica

White House, Washington, DC

Size isn't the only thing that sets St. Peter's apart. There is simply more of everything— five organs, ten chapels, forty-four altars, and more than four hundred statues. Carvings and mosaics are everywhere. Look up and you'll see marble and gold.

The dome of the basilica is 448 feet tall—
tall enough for two space shuttles to fit under it!
The dome itself is actually two layers—like two
gigantic upside-down bowls, one nested inside
the other. In between the two bowls is a narrow
walkway with a spiral staircase. People can climb
the steps to the top of the dome and look out over
all of Rome. By custom, no other building in the
historic center of Rome is taller than St. Peter's.

Nearly a hundred popes are buried in St. Peter's Basilica. St. Peter's own tomb lies directly under the center of the dome. A few of the dead popes are on display in glass coffins, including Pope John XXIII. He died in 1963 but his body was very well preserved. The hands and face are covered in wax. Most of the popes are buried in the crypt, called the grottoes—an underground tomb filled with marble caskets. Visitors can wander among the coffins made of marble or glass and gold. Some of the caskets have life-size marble carvings of the dead pope lying on top.

Only six women are buried in St. Peter's. The most famous one is Christina, who was once the queen of Sweden. She was beloved by the church because she gave up being queen to become a Catholic.

Perhaps the most famous work of art in St. Peter's is a statue called the *Pietà*. It took Michelangelo two years to carve it. The life-size sculpture is of Mary holding the dead body of her son, Jesus. It stands just inside the entrance of St. Peter's and is one of the first things visitors see.

A different sculpture draws just as much attention from faithful visitors. It is the bronze

statue of St. Peter himself. St. Peter is seated on a chair on a raised platform. Worshippers have touched and kissed his foot for centuries—

Pietà at St. Peter's Basilica

so much that the foot is nearly worn away! His toes have disappeared from having been rubbed so often. On June 29 each year, there is a holiday called the Feast of St. Peter and St. Paul. The statue is dressed in holy robes, a ring, and a priceless papal tiara.

At the far end of the church, in the apse, stands St. Peter's throne. It's actually a wooden chair encased inside a bronze and gold one. The wooden chair was thought to be the one St. Peter sat in when he preached.

Statue of St. Peter

Behind the throne is an enormous window in the shape of a sunburst. It looks like stained glass, but it's not. There is no stained glass in St. Peter's. The window is made of thin sheets of a stone called alabaster. It lets light shine through.

With so much gold, marble, and bronze in the basilica, it might seem like the Vatican put all of its wealth into this one spectacular church.

But St. Peter's is just the beginning of the treasures that lie inside the Vatican walls.

CHAPTER 6
Treasures of the Vatican

Beyond the magnificent church, the Vatican is filled with almost too many treasures to imagine or describe.

For hundreds of years, popes collected the best paintings and sculptures they could find. But they were also given priceless gifts of gold, jewels, and clothing. Today, all those treasures are kept in a room right behind the altar of the Sistine Chapel. It is called the Papal Sacristy. There are more than five thousand items altogether.

What treasures are in there?

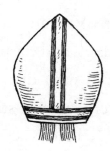

Pope Pius IX's tiara and miter worn by Pope Francis

The most valuable piece is probably the Spanish tiara. Until the twentieth century, popes were crowned with triple tiaras, stacked one on top of the other. Many of the tiaras, made of gold set with gems, are worth millions of dollars. In 1854, Queen Isabella II of Spain gave Pope Pius IX a gold tiara with eighteen thousand diamonds on it! It also had a thousand other precious stones and gems—rubies, emeralds, and pearls. Other popes were given gold and silver tiaras or lavish jewelry. Were the gifts a way to buy the pope's goodwill or favor? Maybe. Today, popes aren't crowned and they don't wear tiaras. Instead, they wear tall hats called miters.

Other Vatican treasures include jeweled crosses, rings, and clasps worn by the popes. Many are covered with diamonds or pearls. There are also tall crosses and staffs that popes use during Mass or religious ceremonies. The staff used by the pope has a cross on top. Other bishops use long staffs with curved tops, like the staff that a shepherd uses to herd his flock of sheep. The pope is said to be the shepherd to all Catholics. The worshippers are his flock.

The treasures of the Vatican don't stop there. Tabletop crosses, cups, bells, candleholders, and many other objects are made from gold or silver. Some of them are decorated with tiny gold depictions of people—less than an inch high—acting out scenes from the Bible.

And then there are the pope's religious clothes, called the papal vestments. Some of the robes are nearly four hundred years old. They are embroidered with gold and colorful silk pictures that look like paintings. Some of the robes took sixteen years to complete.

To celebrate a Mass, the pope also wears a white wool collar or band around his shoulders, with two long tails hanging down. It is called a pallium. The pallium is made of wool from sheep who wear crowns of little red and white flowers on their heads before being sheared!

Is it possible to visit the Vatican and see the many priceless treasures?

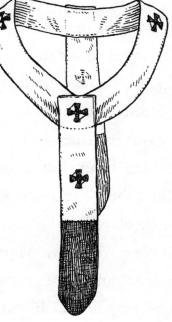

Pallium

Anyone may enter the church, of course.

And tourists and visitors can buy tickets to see the spectacular art in the Vatican museums and the Sistine Chapel.

But treasures in the Papal Sacristy are usually hidden from public view. In 2018, for the first time, the Vatican allowed some of these items to be displayed at the Metropolitan Museum of Art, in New York City. More than a million and a half people came to see the exhibit—the largest crowd a Metropolitan Museum show had ever drawn.

A World Heritage Site

Because of its art, architecture, and museums, Vatican City has been named a World Heritage Site—a place that should never be destroyed or changed. (Other World Heritage Sites include the Great Pyramids and the Statue of Liberty.) The Vatican buildings themselves are works of art. But there are also paintings and sculptures bought or donated throughout the centuries. Many of the statues came from ancient Rome or ancient Egypt. They were carved long before Christianity existed.

All the treasures at the Vatican, and the pope himself, are guarded by members of the Swiss Guard. They are not Catholic priests. They are soldiers. Like the Secret Service agents who protect the president of the United States, they are sworn to give up their lives to defend the Holy Father.

Swiss Guards

The colorful uniforms of the Swiss Guard look like something out of a movie. Wide blue and gold stripes adorn the balloon pants and puffy sleeves. Their helmets sprout red feathers. On some occasions, the guards even wear metal armor. But don't be fooled—the guards are not just for show. They attend military school in Switzerland before coming to the Vatican. Then, at the Vatican, they study martial arts and take combat training. They also learn special drills for ceremonies. They learn how to carry halberds—tall spears with battle axes. The Swiss Guards all live at the Vatican in barracks— military housing.

Sometimes the Swiss Guards are jokingly called the "modesty police." They stand at the entrance to St. Peter's Basilica and make sure each person entering is dressed properly for church. Both women and men must cover their shoulders and clothing must reach the knees.

St. Peter's is a church, not just a tourist site, and people are expected to be quiet and polite inside. But beyond the church and the museums, the Vatican is much more. It contains a whole world of secrets that few people ever get to see.

CHAPTER 7
The Secret Archives

For centuries, popes collected important papers, books, and documents. They were kept in beautiful rooms at the Vatican called the Secret Archives. (An archive is like a library where books and papers about the history of a place are stored.)

The archives were started in 1612 by Pope Paul V. He set aside three rooms in the palace to use as his own private library. Walnut cabinets lined the walls, carved with the pope's coat of arms.

Pope Paul V's coat of arms

Over time, the archives grew in size. Today, there is an enormous underground library, bigger than a stadium. There are thirty thousand parchments in storage. (Parchment is a writing material made from animal skins.) There are also millions of other documents. Some are written on birch bark or silk. There are so many shelves in the archives, if you lined them up in a row, it would be more than fifty miles long!

The Vatican archives aren't really "secret"—they are more like a private library. Scholars are allowed to see most of the papers if they are doing important research. Recent books and letters are kept hidden from the public, though, until the cardinals and popes mentioned in them are long dead. More than a thousand people come to the Vatican every year to study.

Some of the papers in the archives are embarrassing to the Vatican. Why? Because they reveal times when the church did something wrong. One book in the archives tells the story of Galileo Galilei, a scientist in the sixteenth and seventeenth centuries who was wrongly imprisoned. But in 1881, Pope Leo XIII decided to open the archives to the public anyway. He said the church "must not fear the truth."

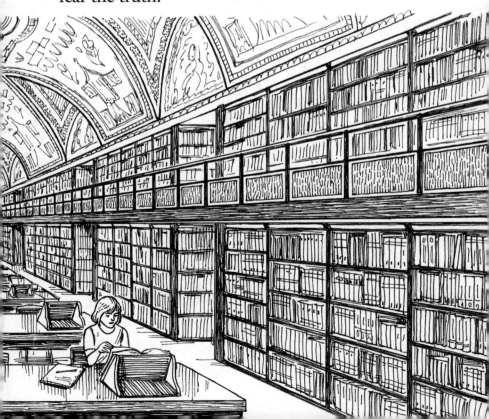

Galileo (1564–1642)

Galileo Galilei was one of the first scientists to understand that the earth moves around the sun. Although Galileo was friends with the pope, the pope became upset because Galileo's ideas seemed to contradict the Bible. Up to this time, people believed that the sun and the other planets moved around the earth. In 1633, the church put Galileo on

trial for his teachings. They forced him to say that his ideas were wrong—even though he knew he was right. Then they kept him locked up in his house for the rest of his life.

The church punished many people over the years for disagreeing with the church's teachings. Sometimes the church even had people killed for their beliefs.

Galileo on trial

One parchment in the Vatican archives is nearly two hundred feet long! It tells the history of the Templar Knights—wealthy knights who fought for the church in the late Middle Ages. It contains many sheets of parchment sewn together and rolled up like a scroll.

Document about Templar Knights found in Vatican archives

In 1926, a man working in the Vatican made an incredible discovery. He was moving an antique wooden chair when he heard something rattling inside. When he looked carefully, he found a secret compartment. Inside was a large parchment, three feet wide. Hanging from the bottom of the letter were eighty-five wax seals attached to red silk ribbons. Each had been stamped with the design from an important person's seal, showing his coat of arms or a picture that identified him. Some were members of the British government. Others were important leaders of the church.

What was this incredible letter?

It was the letter to Pope Clement VII begging him to annul—or cancel—the marriage between Henry VIII and his first wife. Of course, the pope refused to give Henry a divorce. The whole episode changed the history of England forever.

Some of the documents in the Vatican Secret Archives are still not open to the public. Why? They concern things that happened more recently. But Pope Francis has agreed to open the archives sooner for one topic. There are critics who say that during World War II, Pope Pius XII did not speak out against Hitler, the German dictator who murdered millions of Jews. Documents in the archives may show that the Catholic Church did help save thousands of Jews. But papers and letters may also show that Pope Pius XII ignored pleas for help. The letters and documents about

Pope Pius XII will become public on March 2, 2020.

Maybe someday the Vatican will open all the archives for the public to see.

Pope Pius XII

CHAPTER 8
The Vatican in Modern Times

Today, the Vatican is a modern country with its own money, flag, government, and more.

For many years, the official language of the Vatican was Latin—an ancient language no longer spoken. Latin was printed on stamps sold at the Vatican post office. It even popped up on the first screen of automatic teller machines in recent years! Good luck getting your money out if you couldn't read it.

Today, though, Italian has replaced Latin as the official language used on stamps and coins.

For money, the Vatican uses the euro—the same currency used by many European countries. The Vatican's coins have an image of the pope on one side. They are so popular that hardly anyone spends them! People keep the coins as souvenirs.

The flag for Vatican City is square—it is one of only two countries in the world with a square flag. (The other one is Switzerland.) In 1969, the Vatican flag was taken to the moon.

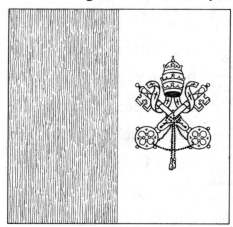

Vatican flag

The Vatican prints its own daily newspaper. And there is also a Vatican radio station and a TV studio as well. The country even has its own special anthem, called the "Pontifical March."

Vatican City is the smallest country in the world—only 109 acres. That's pretty tiny. Disney World is 275 times bigger!

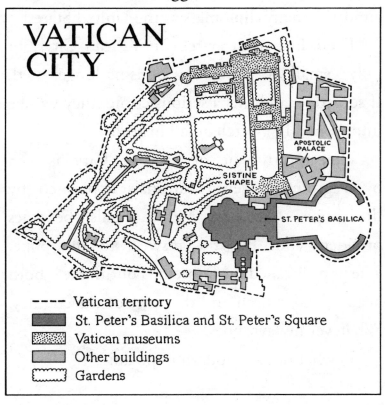

VATICAN CITY

APOSTOLIC PALACE

SISTINE CHAPEL

ST. PETER'S BASILICA

- - - - Vatican territory
St. Peter's Basilica and St. Peter's Square
Vatican museums
Other buildings
Gardens

But even though it's a tiny country, the Vatican plays a role in world affairs. It sends ambassadors to other countries all over the world. In return, other countries send their diplomats to the Vatican. (Diplomats and ambassadors are officials who are sent around the world to represent their country in foreign affairs.) The tiny Vatican has almost as many diplomats as the United States!

There is a court system in Vatican City, but only a small jail—the dungeon is no longer used. If someone commits a serious crime, they will be imprisoned in an Italian jail instead.

The government of Vatican City is run by a group of seven cardinals appointed by the pope. One of the cardinals becomes president, but he still answers to the pope. The pope is called the Supreme Pontiff. He is both head of the church and the ruler of the country. Whatever he says, goes.

So what does a modern pope do?

The pope's job today is to lead the Catholic Church and set an example for Catholics to follow. Modern popes also try to speak out about right and wrong. They try to lead the world in standing up for human rights, even in parts of the world that are not mostly Catholic.

As each new pope is elected, the Catholic world changes a little bit more. In 1962, Pope John XXIII brought about huge changes in the Catholic Church by holding a series of meetings with all the bishops and cardinals.

Pope John XXIII

He invited them to come to Rome four times over a period of three years. They discussed how the church rules should be updated. The meetings were called the Second Ecumenical Council of the Vatican, or Vatican II.

A procession of cardinals entering
St. Peter's Basilica during Vatican II

After Vatican II, the Mass was no longer spoken in Latin. Instead, priests were told to use the common language of wherever they lived. Priests were also allowed to conduct the Mass facing the people instead of facing away from them. And modern music was permitted during the Mass.

A few years later, the pope agreed that Catholics were permitted to eat meat on almost all Fridays. Before 1966, Catholics had been allowed to eat only fish on Fridays.

Vatican II also encouraged Catholics to pray with other Christians and to be friendly toward non-Christians.

But some rules haven't changed even today. Women are still not allowed to become Catholic priests, even though other Christian religions have welcomed women as leaders. The Catholic Church is still controlled by men.

Nuns—women who devote their lives to serving God through the Catholic Church—

are not paid the way priests are paid. Nuns must take a vow of poverty and give any money they earn to the church. But priests and bishops are given a small salary in addition to a place to live, a car, and money for travel.

In the past fifty years, the number of American Catholics who go to church each week has fallen. More than one-third of Americans who were raised Catholic no longer attend church or think of themselves as Catholics. But there are still 1.2 billion Catholics in the world who belong to the church. Most of them live in Latin America, Europe, and Africa. One of the pope's jobs is to reach out to Catholics everywhere and encourage them to stay connected to the church.

One way the Vatican welcomes the world is

by opening the doors of St. Peter's to the public. Several Masses are held almost every day at various chapels inside the basilica.

All are welcome to enter this special place in the world. They cross the border from Italy into Vatican City by simply walking into St. Peter's Square.

But few people will ever see the rest of the pope's private world—the world beyond the church and the museums, where the pope goes about his daily life.

CHAPTER 9
The Pope's Private World

Beyond St. Peter's, there are gardens, a government palace, a grocery store, a bank, a railroad station, churches, a guesthouse, and more. There are more than forty buildings altogether. This is the private world of Vatican City. Only a few hundred people actually live in Vatican City. But about eight hundred people work there every day.

Vatican City railroad station

Who gets to live at the Vatican?

Besides the pope, 110 Swiss Guards live there full-time. Cardinals and priests who run the government also live in Vatican City. And a few workers who take care of the buildings and grounds—electricians, gardeners, and handymen—are full-time residents of the smallest country in the world.

Even though few women live in Vatican City, some nuns are allowed to live in a convent inside the Vatican. A convent is a religious home for nuns. Nuns cook most of the food served to the pope. And nuns run a program to serve meals to homeless men every day. The men line up on the street beside a small door in the Vatican wall. When the door opens, they enter and eat meals served in a simple dining room.

After supper, the men are invited to gather in a chapel for evening prayers.

Other than nuns, there are only a few other women living in Vatican City. They are the wives and children of men who live there full-time. The children go to school outside the Vatican in Rome, but they are sometimes allowed to bring their friends back home to play.

Hundreds of other people come to work at Vatican City every day. Some are artists or experts trained to take care of the paintings and sculptures. There is also a whole studio devoted to making and repairing mosaics—pictures made from small bits of pottery, stone, or glass. Antique furniture experts are in charge of repairing anything made of wood. Other workers build chairs used for events in St. Peter's Basilica. Still other people are in charge of polishing the jewels on the pope's golden miters.

Who else comes to the Vatican to work? Young boys from the Sistine Chapel Choir come to sing for special Masses or ceremonies.

In addition to the Swiss Guards who live there, Vatican City has a regular police force. A small fire department and a first-aid team are also part of the city. They are on hand in case visitors become ill or need help.

And many people work at the radio station and television studio, the grocery store, the library, the museums, the bank, the post office, and in the gardens.

The Vatican gardens cover nearly half the area of the entire country. With fountains, an orchard, tall hedges, and green lawns, the gardens have often been a favorite place for a pope to walk. The public can only visit the gardens as part of a tour group. When the pope wants to stroll through the gardens, visitors are kept out so that the pope can have peace and privacy.

A road runs through the gardens but most Vatican workers and residents use bicycles to get

around, or they walk. There are also tennis courts and a canteen—a place for Vatican workers to eat lunch or dinner.

A small grocery store sells food only to people who live or work at the Vatican—it isn't open to the public. Milk in the store comes from the pope's own cows in the country at Castel Gandolfo. A pharmacy supplies medicines and drugstore items to Vatican workers. There is also a three-story department store for Vatican employees.

There's a railroad station for trains delivering heavy goods to the Vatican. But when the pope wants to leave the Vatican, he doesn't go by train— it's not that kind of train station. Instead, he travels locally in a car nicknamed the Popemobile. And when the pope flies to other cities, whatever plane he's on is called "Shepherd One."

The "Popemobile"

Another thing not many know about is—a secret passageway! Called the Passetto di Borgo, it leads directly from the pope's apartments to a fortress where, in earlier times, the pope could be safe. The Passetto is really a raised tunnel—like a walkway on top of a wall. It is the path Pope Clement VII used when he was under attack in 1527. Many Swiss Guards died trying to protect him as he fled.

The Passetto

In recent years, most popes have lived in an apartment in the Apostolic Palace. But when Pope Francis was elected in 2013, he made a different choice. Instead of the palace, he chose to live in a five-story guesthouse—like a hotel— right beside St. Peter's Basilica.

Pope Francis's bedroom

Domus Sanctae Marthae

The guesthouse is called Domus Sanctae Marthae. It has more than 130 individual rooms for visiting priests and guests. It was built to hold all the cardinals who come to the Vatican for a conclave. During the conclave, cardinals sleep in the guesthouse at night. In the daytime, they walk to the Sistine Chapel, where they are locked in.

Pope Francis decided to live in the simpler guesthouse because he said he preferred to live among people rather than being off by himself.

He eats many of his meals in the common dining room there. And each morning, he holds Mass in the chapel in the Domus. Workers from the Vatican—gardeners and garbage collectors dressed in orange vests and green work clothes—attend the service with him.

It is just one way that the pope reaches out to the people in his flock, so he can touch their lives.

CHAPTER 10
A Year in the Life of a Pope

Throughout most of the year, the pope keeps a busy schedule.

To start the day, the pope wakes up early each morning and celebrates Mass in one of the small chapels within the Vatican. Then he has breakfast. Afterward, he gets to work, reading and writing letters or speeches. Many afternoons, the pope meets with world leaders or other visitors. And then part of each day is spent in prayer. Popes also spend a lot of time talking to cardinals who run the government. There is always a lot to do, dealing with issues in the Catholic Church.

Every Wednesday when he is in Rome, the pope meets with people who have arranged to have an "audience with the pope." In warm

Pope Francis meets with former US president Barack Obama

weather, the audience is held in St. Peter's Square and thousands may attend. During the audience, the pope gives short Bible readings or teachings. Then he prays with the people who have come.

At noon every Sunday, the pope appears at a window that overlooks St. Peter's Square. From there, he gives a short speech and then a blessing to the crowd below. It's the one time each week when the faithful can see the pope in person if they come to Rome.

The pope also conducts several Masses in

St. Peter's Basilica throughout the year. Tickets for Papal Masses are always free, but people must sign up in advance, and far in advance for the two most special holidays—Christmas and Easter. Christmas celebrates the birth of Jesus. Easter marks the day that Christians believe Jesus rose from the dead after being crucified.

On Christmas Eve, the pope holds a special midnight Mass that is shown on television throughout the world. Thousands of people are given seats inside St. Peter's. Tens of thousands of people attend the Mass outdoors, standing in St. Peter's Square. A life-size nativity scene lies next to an enormous Christmas tree. The Mass is filled with music.

Easter services are just as elaborate. The entire week leading up to Easter is carefully planned. On Palm Sunday—the Sunday before Easter— the basilica is filled with priests carrying olive branches, the symbol of peace. On Wednesday, the pope holds a special Mass in St. Peter's for all the employees of the Vatican. On Easter Sunday, up to eighty thousand worshippers crowd into St. Peter's Square to hear the pope give his Bible reading and blessing.

Most modern popes make time for travel to other countries throughout the year. It is part of the job, spreading the religion to distant countries so that Catholics everywhere can feel connected to the church.

But no matter where the pope is—in his small rooms behind the Vatican walls or traveling the world to spread the word of Christianity—he is always doing just one job. He is leading the Catholic Church into the future—which means preserving the traditions of the past while also welcoming change.

Timeline of the Vatican

c. AD 64	St. Peter is crucified in Rome
64–312	Christians are officially persecuted for their religious beliefs
313	Emperor Constantine allows Christians to worship freely
c. 319	Construction begins on the first St. Peter's Basilica
848–852	Pope Leo IV builds a wall around the Vatican
904	Pope Leo V is imprisoned in the Vatican dungeon and killed
1305	Pope Clement V feels unsafe in Rome and moves to France
1506	First stone laid for a new St. Peter's Basilica, completed 120 years later
1508–1512	Michelangelo paints the ceiling of the Sistine Chapel
1517	Martin Luther writes a letter to protest the church's actions
1527	Rome is attacked by enemy soldiers and the Vatican is looted
1612	Pope Paul V builds the Vatican's Secret Archives
1633	The Catholic Church puts Galileo on trial
1870	The Italian army takes over Rome, and popes become "prisoners" in the Vatican
1929	Vatican City becomes its own city-state
1962–1965	Meetings called "Vatican II" held to discuss church rules
2013	Pope Francis elected
2018	Treasures of the Vatican are displayed in New York's Metropolitan Museum of Art

Timeline of the World

c. AD 70	The Colosseum is planned by the emperor Vespasian in Rome
c. 570	Muslim prophet Muhammad is born in Mecca
800	Charlemagne is crowned Holy Roman Emperor in Rome
1478	King Ferdinand II and Queen Isabella I of Spain form the Spanish Inquisition, a court that punishes people for not following the Catholic Church
1534	Henry VIII breaks away from the Catholic Church and forms the Church of England
1564	William Shakespeare is born
1654	Christina, queen of Sweden, gives up her throne to become Catholic
1791	The US Constitution is amended with the Bill of Rights; the First Amendment guarantees religious freedom
1870	Italy becomes a unified country
1896	First modern Olympic Games are held in Athens, Greece
1939	Hitler begins attacks in Europe that lead to World War II
1960	John F. Kennedy is elected first Catholic president of the United States
1964	Michelangelo's *Pietà* sculpture from St. Peter's Cathedral is on view at the World's Fair in New York City
2018	Women in Saudi Arabia are allowed to drive for the first time

Bibliography

*Books for young readers

Arend, Paul den. *Guide to the Vatican: Including Saint Peter's Basilica and the Vatican Museums.* Haren, The Netherlands: VandiDesign, 2014.

Collins, Michael. *The Vatican: Secrets and Treasures of the Holy City.* New York: Dorling Kindersley, 2008.

Graham-Dixon, Andrew. *Michelangelo and the Sistine Chapel.* New York: Skyhorse Publishing, 2016.

*Kirby, Jeffrey. *101 Surprising Facts about St. Peter's and the Vatican.* Charlotte, NC: Saint Benedict Press, 2015.

"Life in the Domus Sanctae Marthae," **Inside the Vatican**, May 1, 2013. https://insidethevatican.com/news/life-in-the-domus-sanctae-marthae/.

Pollett, Andrea. "The Walls of the Popes," **Virtual Roma.** roma.andreapollett.com/S4/vatic11.htm.

St. Peter's Basilica.Info, "St. Peter's Basilica Interactive Floor Plan." stpetersbasilica.info/floorplan.htm.

Websites

w2.vatican.va/content/vatican/en.html

www.vaticanstate.va/content/vaticanstate/en.html